TOOLS FOR CAREGIVERS

- **F&P LEVEL:** A
- **WORD COUNT:** 27
- **CURRICULUM CONNECTIONS:** shapes, community

Skills to Teach

- **HIGH-FREQUENCY WORDS:** a, an, I, see
- **CONTENT WORDS:** circle, diamond, octagon, rectangle, square, triangle
- **PUNCTUATION:** periods
- **WORD STUDY:** long e, spelled *ee* (*see*); *r*-controlled vowel (*circle*); multisyllable words (*diamond, octagon, rectangle, triangle*)
- **TEXT TYPE:** information report

Before Reading Activities

- Read the title and give a simple statement of the main idea.
- Have students "walk" though the book and talk about what they see in the pictures.
- Introduce new vocabulary by having students predict the first letter and locate the word in the text.
- Discuss any unfamiliar concepts that are in the text.

After Reading Activities

This book introduces and points out the shapes we see on signs around our towns, cities, or communities. What shapes can students identify around them in the classroom, school, park, or playground? On the board, draw each shape mentioned in the book. Have readers name objects of those shapes. Start a list next to each shape.

Tadpole Books are published by Jump!, 5357 Penn Avenue South, Minneapolis, MN 55419, www.jumplibrary.com

Copyright ©2020 Jump!. International copyright reserved in all countries. No part of this book may be reproduced in any form without written permission from the publisher.

Editor: Jenna Trnka **Designer:** Anna Peterson

Photo Credits: SageElyse/Shutterstock, cover (circle); Sean Locke Photography/Shutterstock, cover (triangle); Kaspri/Shutterstock, cover (octagon), 2tl, 2mr, 5, 13; Harris Shiffman/Dreamstime, 1; Sergey Novikov/Dreamstime, 3 (girl), 4–5; CynthiaAnnF/iStock, 3 (background); Karenr/Dreamstime, 3 (sign); Art Konovalov/Shutterstock, 6–7; Nemanja Cosovic/Shutterstock, 2bl, 7; Mariusz Blach/Dreamstime, 8–9 (deer); wakr10/iStock, 8–9 (background); ollo/iStock, 2br, 9; Andrei Ksenzhuk/Shutterstock, 10–11; Technicsorn Stocker/Shutterstock, 2tr, 11; Oleksandra Loyish/Dreamstime, 12–13; Special View/Shutterstock, 14–15 (background); DarthArt/iStock, 14–15 (car); Sergey02/Dreamstime, 2ml, 15; TB studio/Shutterstock, 16.

Library of Congress Cataloging-in-Publication Data
Names: Peterson, Anna C., 1982– author.
Title: Let's learn shapes / by Anna C. Peterson.
Description: Minneapolis, MN: Jump!, Inc., 2020. | Series: Fun first concepts | Includes index. | Audience: Ages 3–6.
Identifiers: LCCN 2019031312 (print) | LCCN 2019031313 (ebook) | ISBN 9781645273202 (hardcover) | ISBN 9781645273219 (paperback) ISBN 9781645273226 (ebook)
Subjects: LCSH: Shapes—Juvenile literature. | Street signs—Juvenile literature.
Classification: LCC QA445.5 .P464 2020 (print) | LCC QA445.5 (ebook) | DDC 516/.15—dc23
LC record available at https://lccn.loc.gov/2019031312
LC ebook record available at https://lccn.loc.gov/2019031313

FUN FIRST CONCEPTS

LET'S LEARN SHAPES

by Anna C. Peterson

TABLE OF CONTENTS

WORDS TO KNOW

circle

diamond

octagon

rectangle

square

triangle

sign

I see a circle.

I see a square.

deer

I see a triangle.

I see a diamond.

I see a rectangle.

car

I see an octagon.

LET'S REVIEW!

What shapes do you see below?

INDEX